Forces in Act

By the end of this book you will know more about:
- Push and pull forces.
- Gravity and air resistance.
- How to measure forces.

You will:
- Plan and carry out a fair test.
- Draw line graphs and interpret data.
- Measure different forces.
- Research using CD-ROMs and the Internet.

Task 1 What do forces do?

A force is a push or a pull. It can change the shape of some things.

The bigger the push or pull force, the further something moves or the more the shape of something is changed.

A force can make things slow down, go faster, start or stop.

A pull force can stretch things.

Magnets can push or pull magnetic materials.

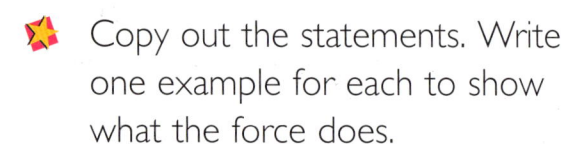

⭐ Read the statements about forces.

⭐ Copy out the statements. Write one example for each to show what the force does.

For example:

A push or a pull force can change the shape of some things.

Sitting on an ice cream will change its shape.

Words to learn and use:
force
magnet

Task 2 It's magnetic!

- Collect some magnets and objects from the classroom.
- What can you remember about magnets?
- Discuss your ideas in your group.

Think about:
- What happens when you place magnets near objects made of different materials?
- Do all metals behave the same way?
- What happens when you hold two magnets together, north to north? South to north? South to south?

- Make a class poster showing your ideas. You could use a computer.

you need:
- magnets
- different objects (metal, plastic, wood)

A push force compresses a spring and a pull force stretches a spring.

Task 3

How far will it go?

- What do you feel when you compress a spring? Try it.

- Write a description of the forces you feel when you compress a spring.

This spring has been compressed, or squashed.

This spring has been expanded, or stretched.

- What do you feel when you stretch or expand a spring? Try it.

- Write a description of the forces you feel when you stretch a spring.

- How does hanging objects of different mass affect the stretch of an elastic band?

- Look at the table. What pattern can you see?

Object	Mass of object (g)	Stretch of elastic band (cm)
pencil	20	10
spoon	58	24
jug	80	35
scissors	90	37
cup	110	45

Use a Newton meter.

Task 4

Scientific Enquiry
What is the pull?

1

Newton meters or forcemeters are used to measure the amount of pull on an object. You could call them a pull force meter. Newton meters measure the pull force in newtons (N).

- Look at the different Newton meters. Which would you use to measure the pull force needed to make these objects start to move?

  chair   book   shoe   brick

- Fill in the second column of the table on Task Sheet 1.

- Measure the pull force needed to make the objects start to move and complete the table on Task Sheet 1. Were your guesses correct?

- Did everyone in your class get the same readings?

you need:
- Newton meters in different ranges (0–2N, 0–5N, 0–10N, 0–20N and 0–50N)
- objects to measure (chair, book, shoe, brick)

Here are some repeat readings Class 6 took.

Object	Pull force 1st reading (N)	2nd reading (N)	3rd reading (N)	Mean average (N)
brick	6	8	8	
shoe	0·75	0·5	1·75	
chair	25	25	24	

- Why did they take repeat readings?
- Calculate the mean average for each object.

⭐ **Gravity is a pull force between objects. Everything is pulled towards Earth because of gravity.**

Task 5

Gravity on Earth

🔲 2

Gravity is a pull force between us and the Earth. It pulls us towards the centre of the Earth and keeps us from floating into space.

✨ Look at Task Sheet 2. On the first picture draw stick people standing at:

- the North Pole
- the South Pole
- a country to the east (right-hand side) of the UK
- a country to the west (left-hand side) of the UK.

On the second picture draw clouds and rain at:

- the North Pole
- the South Pole
- a country to the east (right-hand side) of the UK
- a country to the west (left-hand side) of the UK.

✨ Share your pictures with other children in your class. Are your pictures the same?

The Earth

Words to learn and use:
compress
expand
gravity
mass
newton

Fact File — Gravity

There is a force between every object on Earth. This force is called **gravity** or **gravitational attraction**. You cannot feel it but there is a force between you and this book – it is pulling you towards each other. Gravity is a pull force, which exists between all objects.

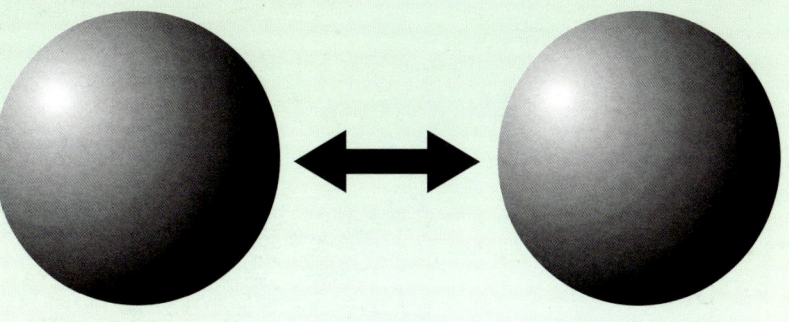

Large masses have a large pull force

Objects that have a large **mass**, or have a lot of stuff in them, such as the Earth and the Moon, have a large pull force. Objects with a smaller mass, or objects that have less stuff in them, have a very small pull force, so small that we are usually not aware of the pull force. The pull force between us and the Earth is the only one that is big enough for us to feel. When objects come closer together, the pull force becomes greater.

Task 6 — More about gravity

- Use CD-ROMs or the Internet to research more information about gravity.

- Make notes of your research then design an A4 leaflet displaying fascinating facts about gravity for other children to read.

Gravity causes objects to have weight. Weight is a force, measured in newtons.

Scientific Enquiry

Task 7

Measuring weight

3

Gravity is a force between us and the Earth. It pulls us towards the centre of the Earth. When you hang an object from a Newton meter, it measures the force of gravity pulling the object down towards the centre of the Earth. Gravity acts upon an object and gives it weight. In outer space where gravity is very weak, objects are almost weightless.

* Measure the pull force of each of your objects using a Newton meter.

* Use Task Sheet 3 to record your findings.

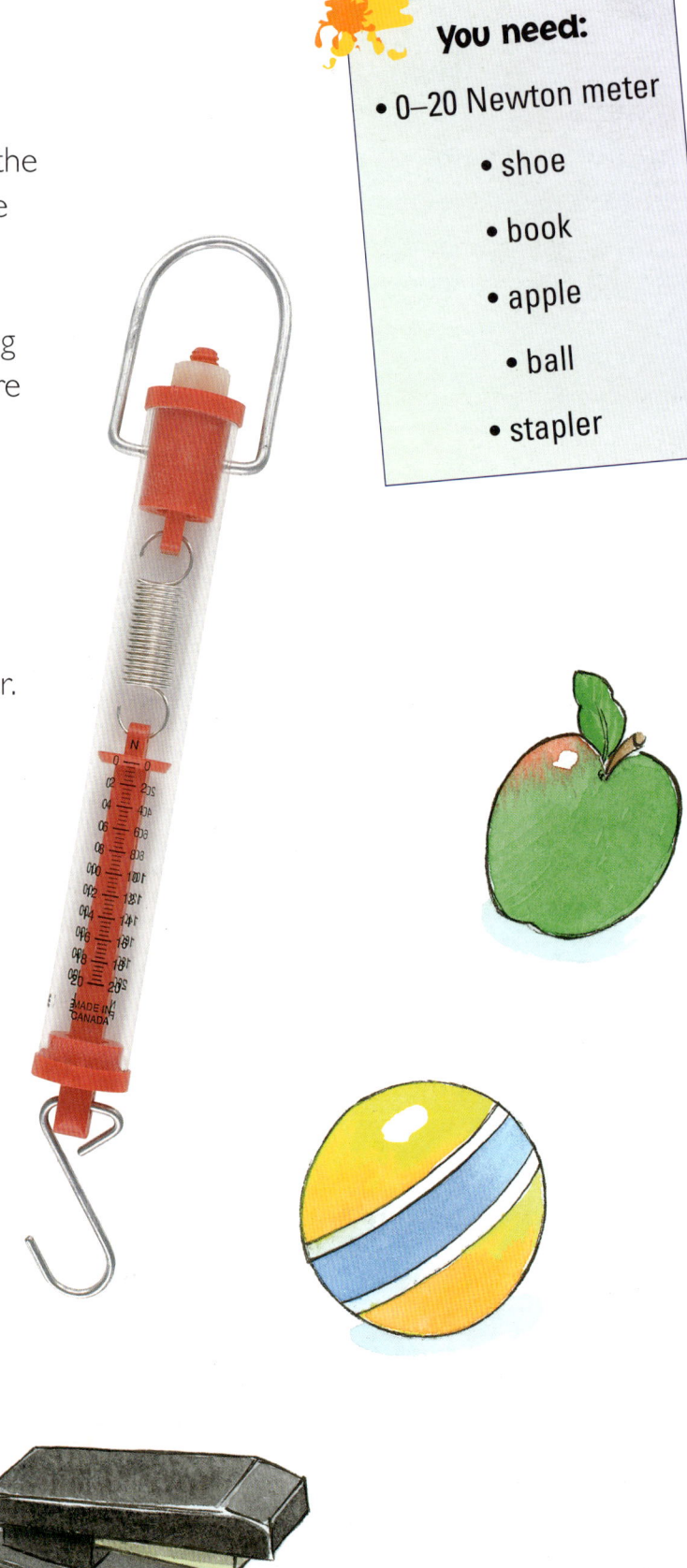

you need:
- 0–20 Newton meter
- shoe
- book
- apple
- ball
- stapler

Task 8: Walking on the Moon

Buzz Aldrin on the Moon

In 1969, Buzz Aldrin was one of the first men to walk on the Moon. Here is what he said about the experience:

"I took off jogging to test my manoeuvrability. The exercise gave me an odd sensation and looked even odder when I later saw films of it. With bulky suits on, we seemed to be moving in slow motion. Earth-bound I would have stopped my run in just one step but I had to use three or four steps to sort of wind down."

★ On the Moon, Buzz Aldrin weighed six times less than on Earth! How does this prove that the force of gravity is less on the Moon than it is on Earth? Explain why you think that.

★ Use CD-ROMs and the Internet to find out more about the first Moon landing.

★ Write your own description of what you think it would be like to walk on the Moon.

Different forces acting on an object can be shown by arrows.

Task 9 Showing forces

4

⭐ Look at the pictures. Can you work out which forces are acting in each one?

⭐ Using Task Sheet 4, draw arrows on each picture to show the direction of the forces.

Task 10

Scientific Enquiry
Feel the push

- Carefully push an inflated balloon into a tank of water.

- What do you feel?

- What is the water doing to the balloon?

- Now let go of the balloon. What happens?

- Draw and write to show what you think is happening when you push the balloon and when you let go of the balloon.

You are using a push force to get the balloon into the water. The water is pushing the balloon back up.
We can use arrows to show the direction of the force.

We use different sized arrows to show which force is bigger – a bigger arrow means a bigger force.

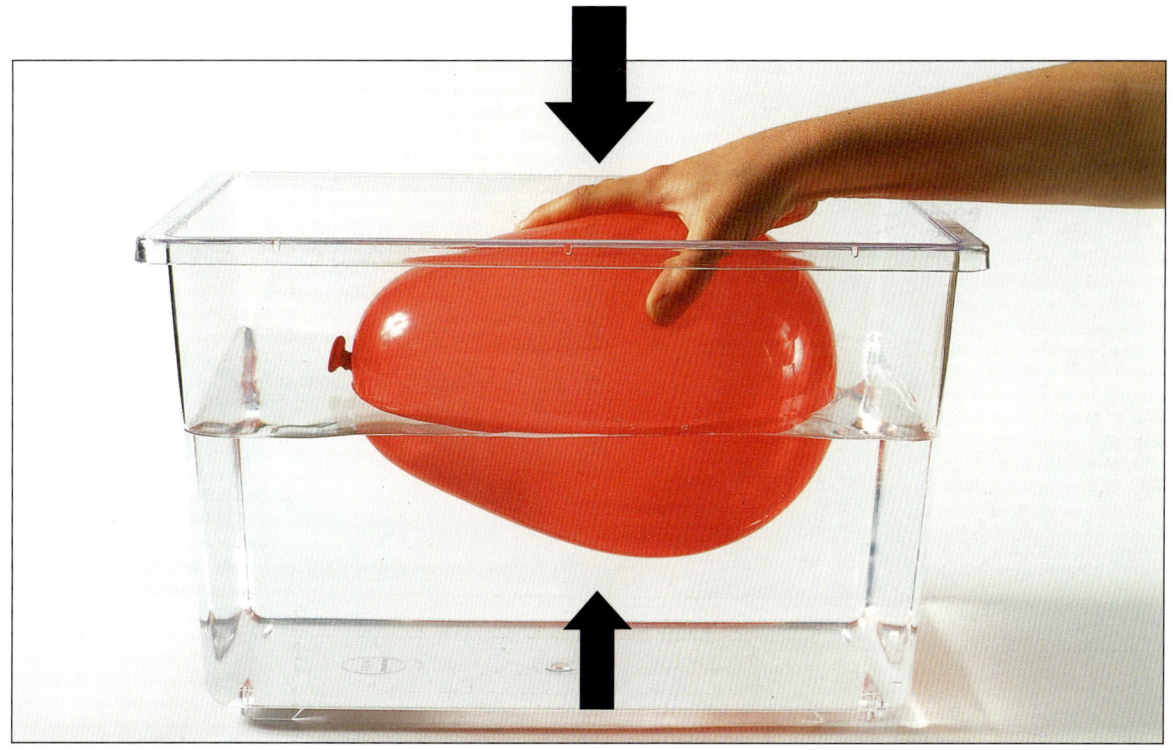

you need:
- plastic tank part filled with water
- inflated balloon

Pushing a balloon into water

⭐ **Water provides an upward force on objects.**

Fact File

The push force of water

When something is pulled or pushed down into water, the water pushes back. This push back is called 'up-thrust'.

When you put a tennis or rubber ball on water, there is the pull of gravity between the ball and the Earth. But at the same time, the water is pushing up on the ball. Gravity pulls downward as the water pushes upward. If the up-thrust of the water and the weight of the object are balanced, then the object floats.

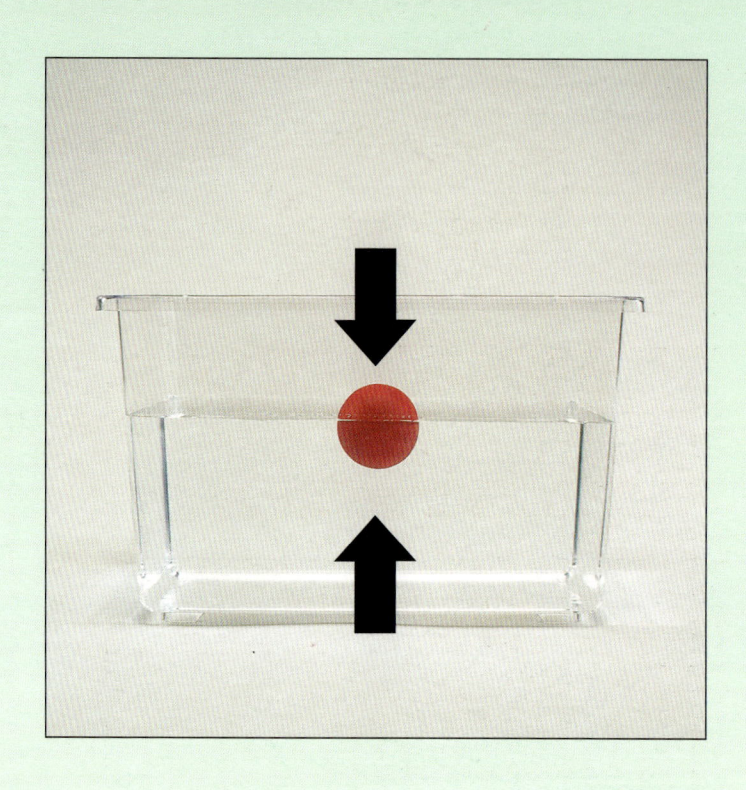

If the weight of the object is greater than the up-thrust of the water, then the object sinks.

The stretch of an elastic band depends on the force acting on it.

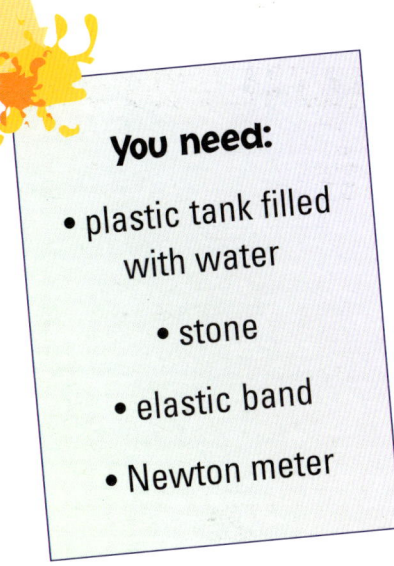

you need:
- plastic tank filled with water
- stone
- elastic band
- Newton meter

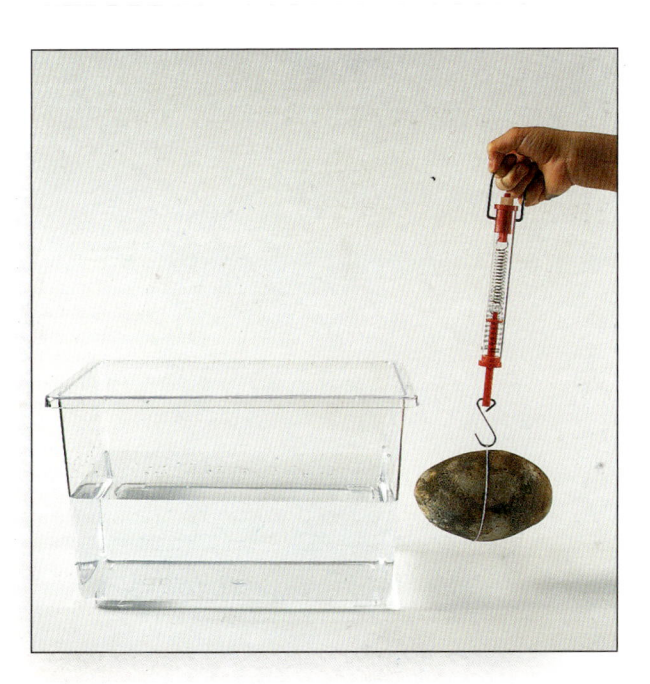

Task 11

Scientific Enquiry

Measuring the push

- Tie the stone to the elastic band. How far does it stretch?

- Now hang the stone in the water.

- What happens to the elastic band?

- Draw a picture to show what you think happens to the stone and the elastic band when you put the stone in the water. Use arrows to help you explain.

- What would you have to do to make the elastic band the same length in air as it is in the water? What does this tell you about what the water is doing?

- Now weigh the stone using a Newton meter. Write down the weight (the pull down towards Earth).

- Keep the stone hooked to the Newton meter and lower the stone into the water.

- The reading on the Newton meter changes. Why do you think this is?

- Record the change. What is the difference?

Do not drop the stone in the tank. It could damage the tank.

⭐ **Check measurements by repeating them.
Use patterns in measurements to explain what is happening.**

Task 12

Scientific Enquiry

What's happening?

You need:
- different objects
- Newton meter
- plastic tank filled with water

You are going to weigh several objects in air and then in water using a Newton meter.

✴ What do you think will happen to the objects in water?

✴ Take a range of measurements, remembering to repeat your readings to make sure your results are reliable.

✴ Use a computer to record your results and draw a graph showing the Newton meter readings in air and in water for your objects. What type of graph will you draw?

✴ What does your graph tell you? Present your results to the class. Remember to explain:

- how you carried out the activity
- why you took repeat readings
- what your results show
- your conclusions.

14

Use results to answer questions and draw conclusions.

You need:
- masses
- elastic bands
- rulers

Task 13

Scientific Enquiry

How far will it stretch?

Class 6 were asked to find out how different masses affect the stretch of an elastic band.

These are some of their ideas before starting their investigation.

Shall we measure the stretch or the whole length of elastic every time?

How will we measure the stretch?

Will we need to take repeat readings? Why?

How will we make sure our test is safe?

When they had finished their investigation, they had to think about their results.

Are we sure of our results? Why?

What kind of graph do we need?

What pattern does it follow?

What is the pattern of the data?

What is our conclusion? How does it link to the data?

⚠️ Take care when using elastic bands that they are not flicked or snapped at anyone. Do not stretch the elastic bands until they break.

15

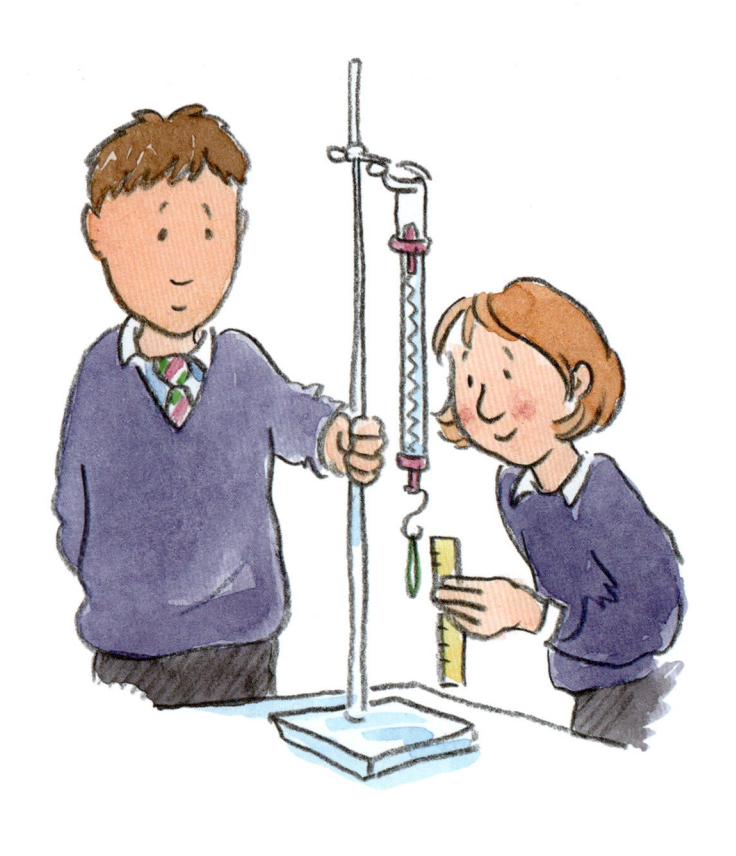

- Carry out Class 6's investigation.
- Use their ideas to help you.
- When you have completed your investigation, use a computer to write a one page fax telling Class 6 what you found out.

⭐ **Falling objects are slowed by air resistance, which acts in the opposite direction to weight.
Identify scientific explanations for results.**

Task 14
Scientific Enquiry
Dropping paper

✦ Write down what you think will happen if you drop two pieces of paper:
- the same size
- from the same height
- at the same time
- one piece crumpled and the other piece flat.

✦ Now try it.

✦ What happened?
Were your ideas correct?

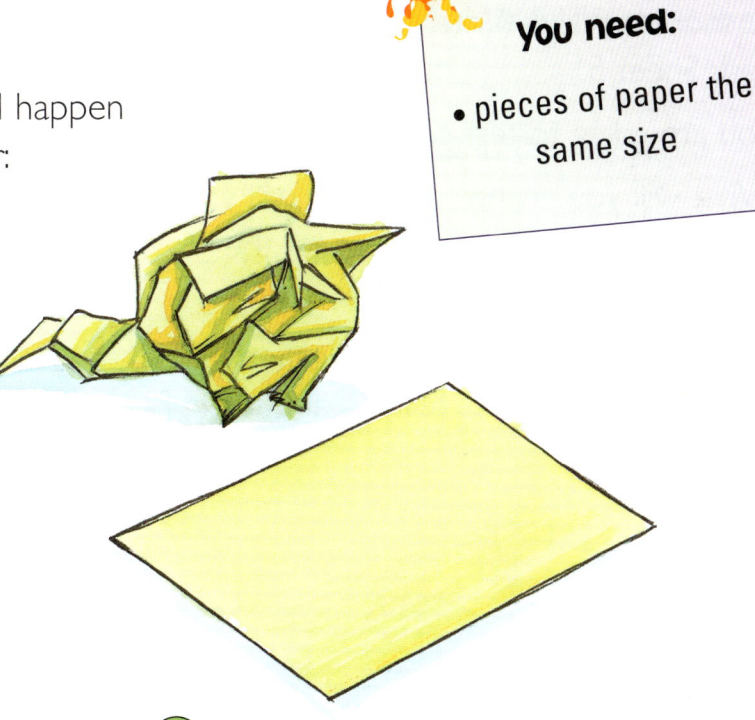

you need:
- pieces of paper the same size

Task 15
Falling parachutes

✦ These are some of Class 5's ideas on how a parachute works.

1 Parachutes work because of air resistance or air friction over the surface of the parachute. The air friction provides a force that is smaller than gravity and acts in the opposite direction to gravity. This slows the parachute.

2 Real parachutes are so big that the person comes down slowly.

3 It is because of air resistance.

4 Air holds the parachute up so that it floats on air.

✦ Write your thoughts on each of their ideas. Are their explanations good?

✦ Which is the best explanation? Why?

17

You are going to draw a graph of your results.

This is the graph Class 6 made to show their results.

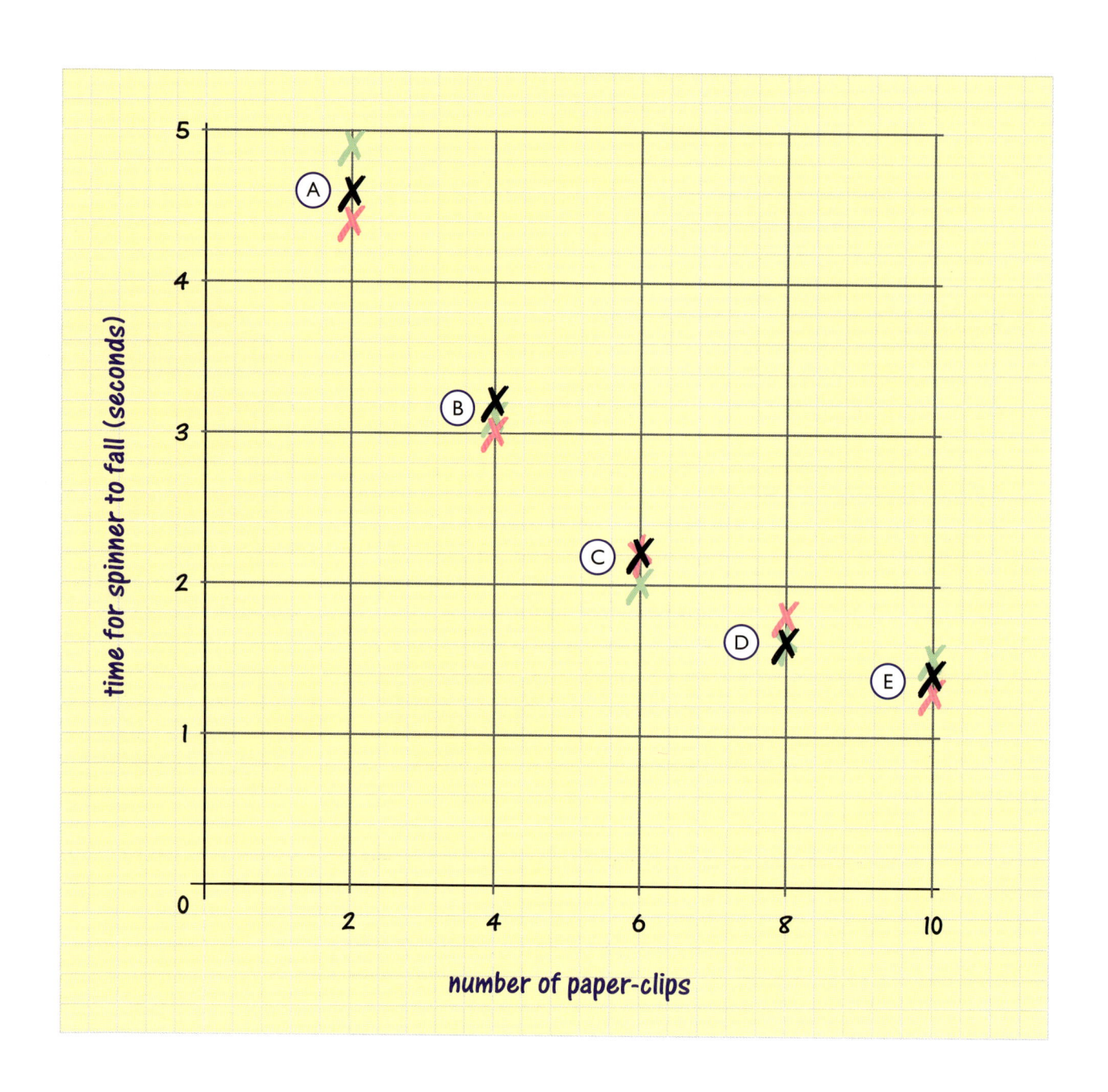

graph: time for spinner to fall (seconds) vs number of paper-clips, with points A, B, C, D, E

- Do you think that all their results can be trusted?

- Look at the first set of results, marked A on the graph. There is quite a large variation. Why do you think this is? Can these results be trusted?

- Look at the results marked C. They are very similar to each other. Can these results be trusted more than the results marked A?

- How could Class 6 make sure that their graph showed only reliable results?

Class 6 took middle readings and plotted them onto a new graph. They thought that joining the points with a line would help them to understand the pattern of results. This is their new graph.

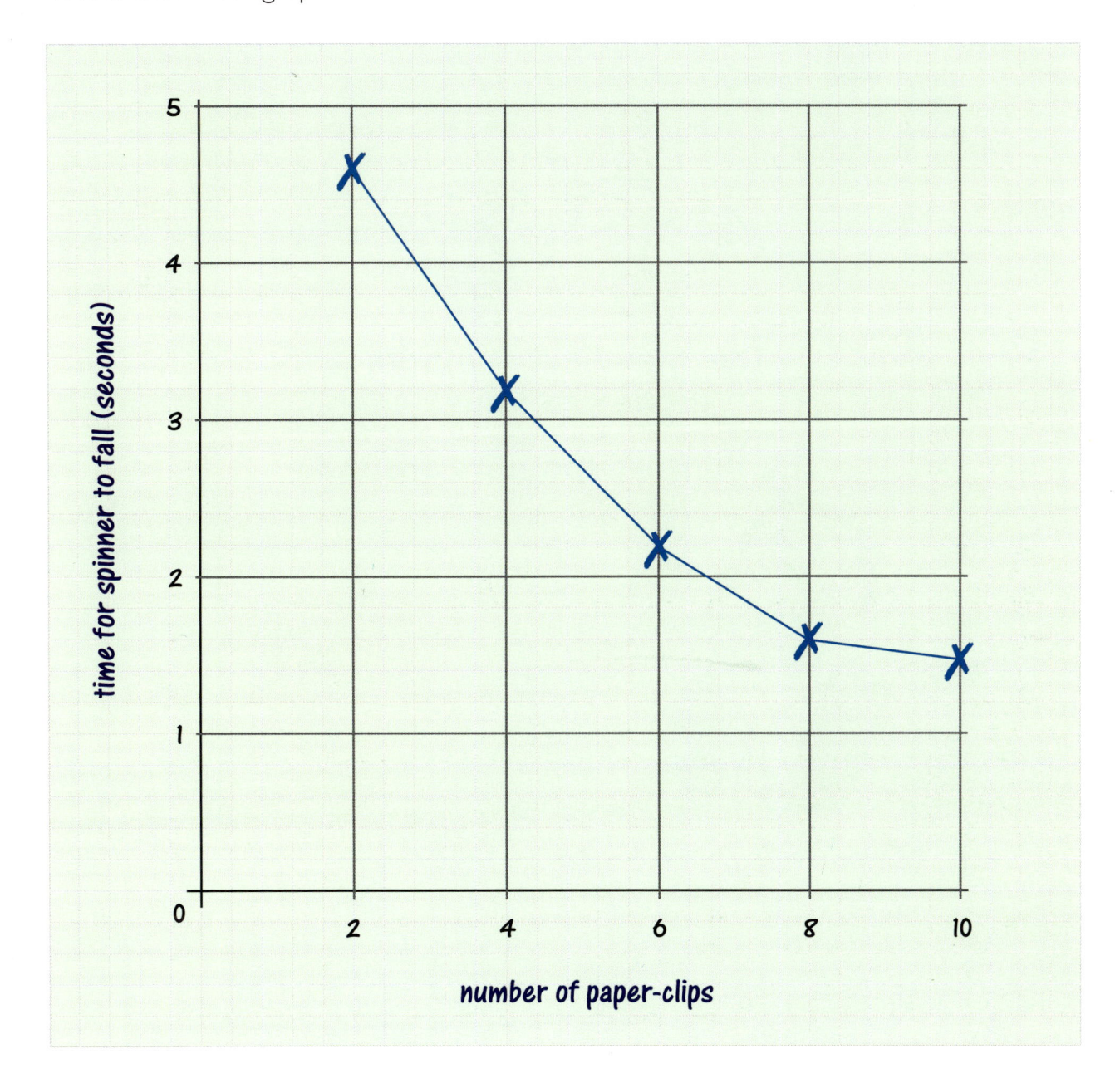

Graph: time for spinner to fall (seconds) vs number of paper-clips

⁂ Look at the line and continue it with your finger. What do you think will happen to the line? Will it go down to touch the axis? Why not?

⁂ Answer the questions on Task Sheet 6.

⁂ Now draw two graphs of your results. One showing all the data, the other showing only the middle readings. What do your graphs tell you?

Words to learn and use:
air resistance
gravity
water resistance

Checkpoint

Forces in action

⭐ Read this newspaper advert for Splendid Spinners.

Splendid Spinners

The speediest spinners money can buy!

The lightest spinners around

Science has shown that spinners made from extra light materials fall faster than normal spinners.

Buy one get one FREE!!

available from:
The Science Spin Company, Spindley

⭐ Is the advert correct? Look back through your work and write a letter to The Science Spin Company telling them what you think of their product. Use the evidence you have collected.

⭐ Copy these pictures and draw arrows to show the direction of the forces in action. Remember to draw bigger arrows to show the biggest forces.

⭐ What are the forces? Label your arrows.

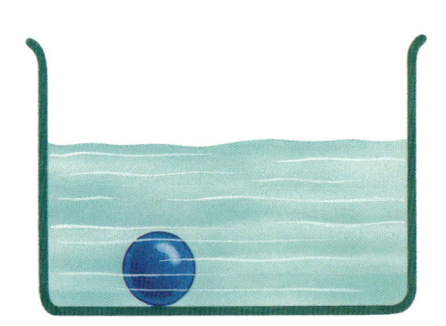

Summary

Which of these do you know and which can you do?

- I know that a push force compresses a spring and a pull force stretches a spring.
- I can use a Newton meter.
- I know that gravity is a pull force between objects. Everything is pulled towards Earth because of gravity.
- I know that gravity causes objects to have weight.
- I know that weight is a force, measured in newtons.
- I know that different forces acting on an object can be shown by arrows.
- I know that water provides an upward force on objects.
- I know that the stretch of an elastic band depends on the force acting on it.
- I can check measurements by repeating them.
- I can use patterns in measurements to explain what is happening.
- I can use results to answer questions and draw conclusions.
- I know that falling objects are slowed by air resistance, which acts in the opposite direction to weight.
- I can identify scientific explanations for results.

Complete your **Science Log** to show how well you know these and how well you can do them. Circle a face for each statement.

Glossary

air resistance

air resistance – a force which slows objects moving through air.

compress – to make smaller or squeeze together.

expand – to make bigger or stretch.

force – a push or pull on an object.

gravity – the pull force between objects such as the Earth and us.

magnet – a metal object that can attract iron or steel.

mass – the amount of a material in a certain amount of space.

newton – a unit of force.

Newton meter – an instrument that measures pull forces or weight.

water resistance – a force that slows objects moving through water.

expand

pull force